W9-BXT-450

SPECIAL OPERATIONS

John Townsend

A+

Smart Apple Media

Published by Smart Apple Media, an imprint of Black Rabbit Books
P.O. Box 3263, Mankato, Minnesota 56002
www.smartapplemedia.com

Published by arrangement with Watts Publishing, London.

Cataloging-in-Publication Data is available from the Library of Congress
ISBN: 978-1-59920-983-8   (library binding)
ISBN: 978-1-68071-003-8   (eBook)

Printed in the United States by CG Book Printers
North Mankato, Minnesota

PO 1727
3-2015

Contents

Secret Missions

When Adolf Hitler's forces invaded Poland in 1939, he began the deadliest conflict in history. World War II lasted for six years. Part of the war was fought by secret forces, including *commandos* and spies. Their work was full of danger.

US Marines land on a beach under fire from artillery *shells.*

Commando units were small fighting forces trained for making quick "hit-and-run" raids in enemy-held areas. In 1940 over 2,000 British men joined a Special Service Brigade that grew into 12 commando units.

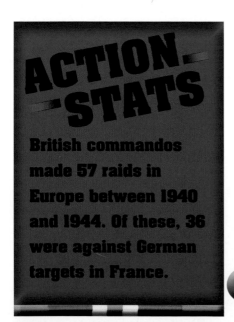

ACTION STATS

British commandos made 57 raids in Europe between 1940 and 1944. Of these, 36 were against German targets in France.

Some special operations units carried out secret raids.

4

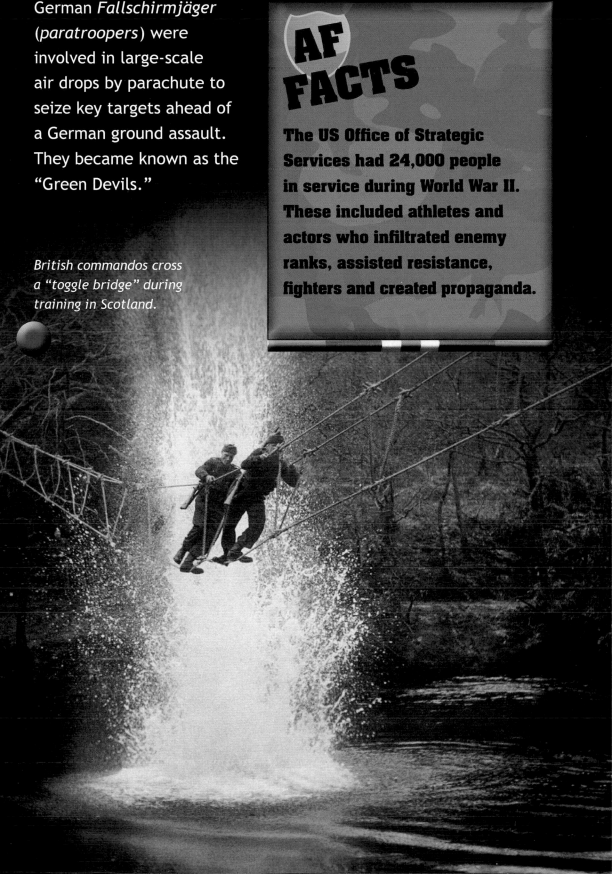

German *Fallschirmjäger* (*paratroopers*) were involved in large-scale air drops by parachute to seize key targets ahead of a German ground assault. They became known as the "Green Devils."

British commandos cross a "toggle bridge" during training in Scotland.

Brandenburgers: German Special Forces

The Brandenburg German Special Forces were set up by Captain Theodor von Hippel. The unit's missions behind enemy lines were to cause maximum damage and confusion.

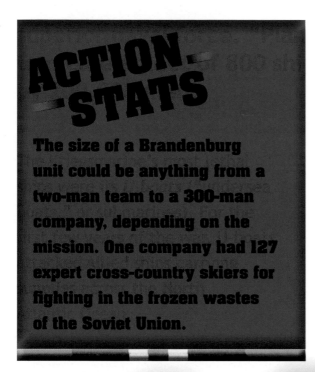

German troops before a raid in Yugoslavia.

All "Brandenburgers" spoke foreign languages and were highly skilled with a variety of weapons. Many trained as pilots and paratroopers. All Brandenburgers carried a suicide pill which they were expected to swallow if they were captured.

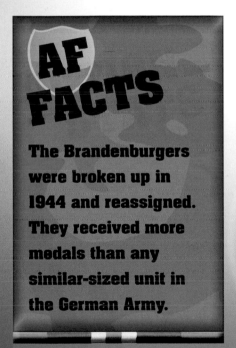

An assault by German forces in frozen conditions in the Soviet Union.

AF FACTS

The Brandenburgers were broken up in 1944 and reassigned. They received more medals than any similar-sized unit in the German Army.

In May 1940, before Germany's main attack on the Netherlands, an eight-man team of Brandenburgers went to capture a bridge in the Dutch town of Gennep. They dressed as Dutch policemen. No one suspected they were German forces until they suddenly attacked. Three of them were wounded but the others secured the bridge.

SOE Spy Force

One *tactic* for stopping an enemy's plans was to find out what the plans were and to *sabotage* them. This was the job of Britain's Special Operations Executive (SOE).

ACTION STATS

Winston Churchill wanted Britain's SOE force to "set Europe ablaze." Of the 13,000 people working for the SOE, about 3,200 were women. Many were captured and killed by German forces.

After Germany invaded France, SOE agents parachuted in to help the *French Resistance*. This involved spying on German troops and trying to destroy their equipment without getting caught.

Members of the French Resistance displaying weapons used in raids against occupying forces.

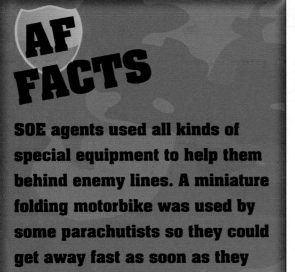

SOE agents used all kinds of special equipment to help them behind enemy lines. A miniature folding motorbike was used by some parachutists so they could get away fast as soon as they landed. Communication radios were hidden in suitcases.

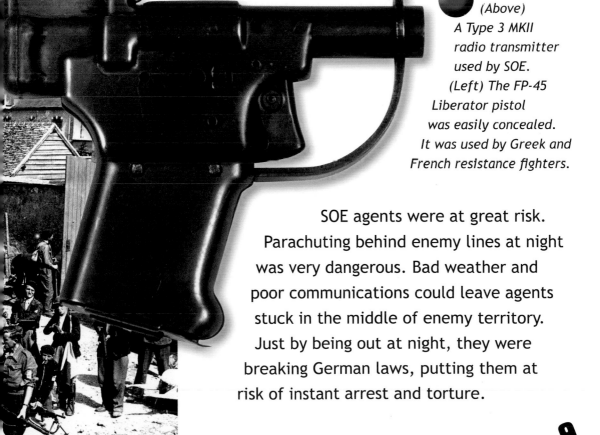

(Above)
A Type 3 MKII radio transmitter used by SOE.
(Left) The FP-45 Liberator pistol was easily concealed. It was used by Greek and French resistance fighters.

SOE agents were at great risk. Parachuting behind enemy lines at night was very dangerous. Bad weather and poor communications could leave agents stuck in the middle of enemy territory. Just by being out at night, they were breaking German laws, putting them at risk of instant arrest and torture.

Strike Forces

Special operations strike forces carried out many daring, high-risk raids during the war. These missions were among the war's most dangerous.

Decima MAS was an Italian special unit that sent *frogmen* on raids to sink enemy ships. In 1941, a small Italian force used explosives to sink Britain's HMS *York* (above), docked in Greece. All six Italian commandos were captured.

An example of a mini sub used by Italian frogmen during their raid on HMS York.

In 1943, Italian soldiers imprisoned their dictator, Mussolini. Germany sent a special unit to rescue him, led by Lieutenant Colonel Otto Skorzeny.

Skorzeny ran daring raids during World War II with his *elite* team (which included ex-Brandenburgers, see pages 6–7). They landed silently by glider and overcame the Italian guards, before flying back to Vienna with Mussolini.

Soviet marine commando special forces in training in the Black Sea area.

Special Air Service Brigade

The British Army's Special Air Service Brigade (SAS) was formed in 1941 by Captain David Sterling. It became one of the war's most successful fighting units.

Men of the Special Air Service returning from a three-month mission behind enemy lines in North Africa, 1942.

At the end of 1941, the SAS went on its first mission. They parachuted behind enemy lines in North Africa to gather information and disrupt German bases.

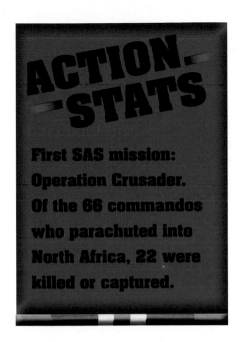
However, bad weather and German attacks led to capture or death for many of the men in this first SAS unit.

Later missions were far more successful. By the end of the war, SAS forces were making a difference. Small units in France worked with the French Resistance to attack railway lines and bridges, as well as gather secret information. This work helped to make the *D-Day* landings in June 1944 a success.

Members of 2nd Special Air Service after parachuting into northern Italy.

US Marine Raiders

After Japanese planes attacked American ships in Pearl Harbor at the end of 1941, the US joined the war on the side of the *Allies*.

US President Franklin Roosevelt ordered the formation of an American version of the British commandos. The best servicemen from the Marine Corps began training for an elite unit named the Marine Raiders.

US Marine Raiders in an amphibious assault craft.

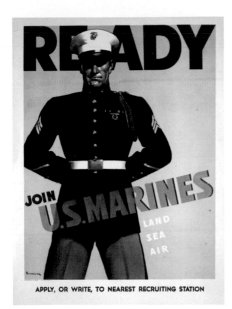

Often, special operations by the Marine Raiders were *amphibious* raids. These secret missions involved landing ashore in small boats or *landing craft* and operating behind enemy lines. Small groups of highly trained Marine Raiders performed many daring strikes from the sea.

Among the first US special operations forces to see combat in World War II were Edson's Raiders of the 1st Marine Raiders *Battalion* and Carlson's Raiders of the 2nd Marine Raiders.

World War II recruitment poster for the US Marines, from which the Raiders were born.

ACTION STATS

Four Marine Raider battalions served in special operations until 1944. A battalion is a unit of between 300 and 1,200 soldiers. Several battalions are grouped to form a *regiment* or a brigade.

Case Study: Raiders in Action

One of the Marine Raiders' famous missions was their attack on Japanese bases on the Gilbert Islands in the Pacific Ocean. Two US submarines, the USS *Nautilus* and USS *Argonaut*, set off from Hawaii with over 200 Raiders on board.

 The submarine *Argonaut in dock before setting off on its mission from Hawaii.*

The task of the Marine Raiders was to land on Makin Island and gather information, destroy enemy bases, and cause a diversion while US troops landed on the Solomon Islands.

AF FACTS

The Marine Corps came under pressure from President Roosevelt to strike back at the Japanese after Pearl Harbor. The Makin raid on August 17, 1942 was designed to show that the US could still attack the Japanese.

As soon as they landed on Makin Island in their boats, the Raiders were in trouble. Exact details of the operation had changed but not all the men were told. One unit worked with the old plans, so there was confusion, especially when trying to get back to the submarines. Nine men were left behind after the submarines set off. All nine were caught by the Japanese and beheaded.

ACTION STATS

As result of the Makin raid, 30 Marine Raiders and over 150 Japanese troops were killed. The mission destroyed the Japanese base on the island.

Marines invade Makin Island, December 13, 1943.

US Rangers

World War II also saw action for the US Rangers. Their role was to strike behind enemy lines. They quickly earned the motto: "Rangers lead the way!"

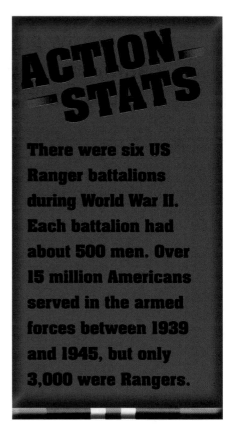

ACTION STATS

There were six US Ranger battalions during World War II. Each battalion had about 500 men. Over 15 million Americans served in the armed forces between 1939 and 1945, but only 3,000 were Rangers.

US Rangers scale ladders to reach German gun positions on top of cliffs, June 6, 1944.

During World War II the US Rangers were formed by Lieutenant Colonel William O. Darby. He trained with his volunteers at the Commando Training Depot at Achnacarry Castle, Scotland. Training was tough. Recruits had to go on speed marches carrying heavy logs. They also climbed cliffs, practiced amphibious assaults, and learned hand-to-hand fighting. Each trainee had to pass the "death slide" test. That meant climbing to the top of a high tree and sliding down a rope over a raging river—all while under fire from live ammunition!

AF FACTS

In 1942, the US Rangers began making raids behind enemy lines as well as amphibious raids on enemy-held coasts. Many of the men in the Darby's Rangers task force were killed in Italy.

US Rangers lead an attack on enemy positions in Italy, 1943.

US Rangers on the death slide.

Operation Frankton: Cockleshell Heroes

When spies saw German ships in the French river port of Bordeaux, British commandos went into action. A small unit of Royal Marines set off on a special operation, code-named Operation Frankton.

Under cover of darkness, 12 marines arrived by submarine at the mouth of the Gironde River. They paddled miles upstream, in kayaks called "cockleshells," toward Bordeaux. The plan was to place mines under the docked German ships and then escape overland to Spain.

A film still from the movie The Cockleshell Heroes *showing commandos setting off from their submarine.*

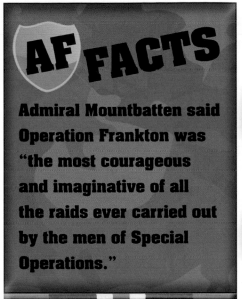

A six-magnet limpet mine, like the ones used during Operation Frankton.

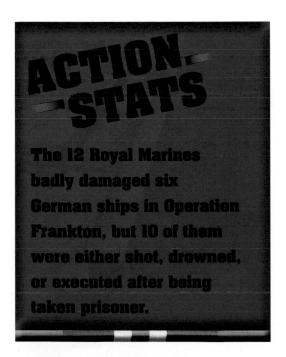

Six kayaks took two men each, with their *limpet mines*, hand grenades, six-day rations, wrenches to set the mines, and magnets to hold the kayaks against the ships.

The marines (later named the Cockleshell Heroes) had pistols and knives, but these were of little use when German troops caught them. Only two men escaped back to Britain.

Devil's Brigade

The 1st Special Service Force (1st SSF) was a joint American-Canadian commando unit. It was set up in 1942 to go on daring missions in Europe.

Members of 1st SSF became known as the "Black Devils," possibly because of the black boot polish they smeared on their faces for secret night-time operations. Their first special operation, code-named Project Plough, was to parachute into German-held Norway to knock out key targets such as power stations.

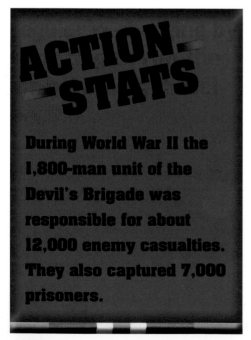

Devil's Brigade commandos in training in the Rocky Mountains.

ACTION STATS

During World War II the 1,800-man unit of the Devil's Brigade was responsible for about 12,000 enemy casualties. They also captured 7,000 prisoners.

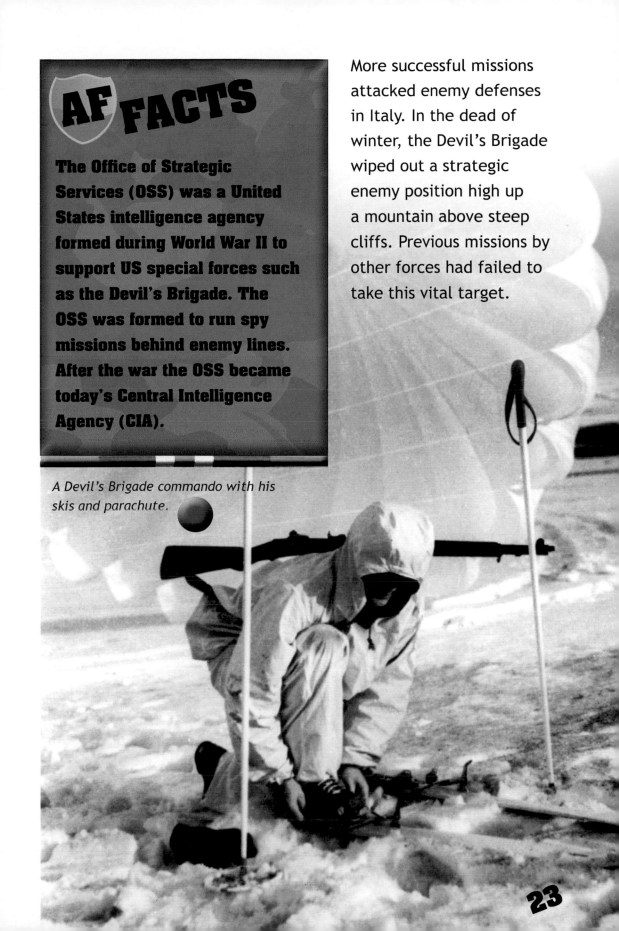

The Office of Strategic Services (OSS) was a United States intelligence agency formed during World War II to support US special forces such as the Devil's Brigade. The OSS was formed to run spy missions behind enemy lines. After the war the OSS became today's Central Intelligence Agency (CIA).

More successful missions attacked enemy defenses in Italy. In the dead of winter, the Devil's Brigade wiped out a strategic enemy position high up a mountain above steep cliffs. Previous missions by other forces had failed to take this vital target.

A Devil's Brigade commando with his skis and parachute.

Operation Jaywick: Z Special Unit

Australia's Z Special Unit carried out commando raids against Japanese troops around the Pacific. One of these raids against Japanese ships in Singapore harbor in 1943 was code-named Operation Jaywick.

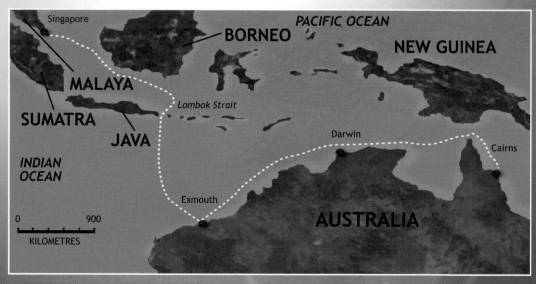

A small unit sailed from Australia in an old fishing boat called MV *Krait*. The men onboard were disguised as fishermen as they headed toward Singapore 1,680 miles (2,700 km) away. Over three weeks later they reached Subor Island, 7 miles (11 km) from Singapore.

 A map showing the route taken by Z Special Unit during Operation Jaywick.

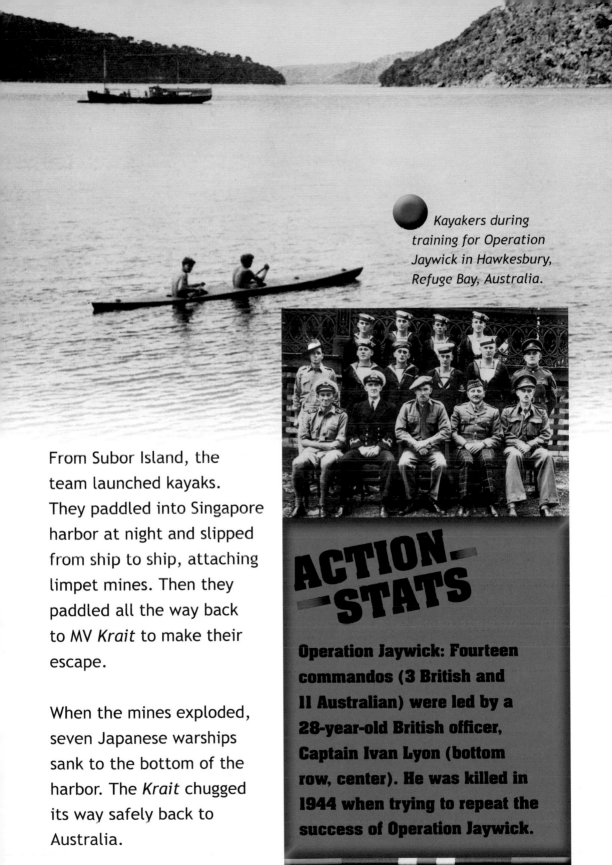

Kayakers during training for Operation Jaywick in Hawkesbury, Refuge Bay, Australia.

From Subor Island, the team launched kayaks. They paddled into Singapore harbor at night and slipped from ship to ship, attaching limpet mines. Then they paddled all the way back to MV *Krait* to make their escape.

When the mines exploded, seven Japanese warships sank to the bottom of the harbor. The *Krait* chugged its way safely back to Australia.

ACTION STATS

Operation Jaywick: Fourteen commandos (3 British and 11 Australian) were led by a 28-year-old British officer, Captain Ivan Lyon (bottom row, center). He was killed in 1944 when trying to repeat the success of Operation Jaywick.

A Japanese machine gunner during an assault training mission.

Japanese Action Force

One of Japan's special forces from the Imperial Japanese Army Air Force (IJAAF) was called the *Teishin Shudan*. Its assault team struck against American bases around the Pacific.

The Teishin Shudan was set up after Japanese commanders saw how successful German paratroopers were during their missions in Europe. The Japanese paratroopers first saw action in 1942, when they successfully captured Palembang airfield on Sumatra.

Japanese paratroopers
descend with parachutes.

Japan formed its Yokosuka
Special Naval Landing
Force (or *Rikusentai*) in
September 1941. Over
2,000 paratroopers were
used for naval assaults and
airborne drops. Yokosuka
paratroopers were involved
in the Borneo campaign
at the Battle of Menado,
and took heavy casualties
during the Battle of Timor.

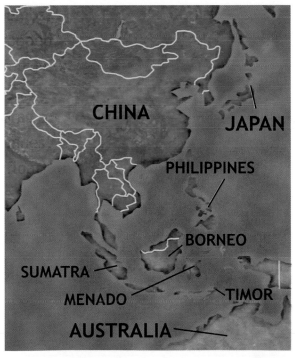

Final Missions

Special Operations played a key part in D-Day, when Allied troops landed in France in huge numbers. For the last months of World War II in Europe, special operations and resistance forces assisted Allied troops as they closed in on Berlin.

Operation Jedburgh

The "Jeds," were units of British, French, and US special forces, working together with members of the Dutch and Belgian armies. They dropped into Europe before D-Day to sabotage German bases and assist Allied troops and local resistance fighters. On one mission, they drained the axle oil from a German train to stop it from transporting tanks.

Night-time drops allowed Jeds to sneak into enemy territory.

Leading up to D-Day, special operations and secret agents were busy with Operation Fortitude. They used fake radio broadcasts to give out false information, and even built camps of fake aircraft and tanks. Spies planted stories and documents with known German agents. All of this was designed to trick German intelligence into thinking that an invasion would happen elsewhere.

Germany was eventually defeated in May 1945, but the war continued in the South Pacific until Japan officially surrendered on September 2.

ACTION STATS

British commandos were awarded 479 decorations during World War II. This included eight *Victoria Crosses*. A commando memorial was unveiled in 1952.

The monument to British commandos, which stands at Spean Bridge, Scotland.

· WE · CONQUER

World War II Timeline

1939: September 1 – Germany invades Poland. World War II begins.

1940: June 10 – Italy joins the war as a member of the Axis powers.

1941: March 26 – Italian commandos sink HMS *York* in Greece.

1941: July – SAS formed in Britain by David Sterling.

1941: December 7 – Japan attacks Pearl Harbor. The US enters the war on the side of the Allies.

1942: August 7 – US Marine Raiders attack Makin in the Gilbert Islands.

1942: October 18 – The Commando Order is issued by Adolf Hitler, stating that all Allied commandos found in Europe and Africa should be killed.

1942: December 7 – The Cockleshell Heroes carry out Operation Frankton in Bordeaux, France.

1943: September 3 – Italy surrenders. German special forces help Mussolini escape.

1943: September 26 – Australia's Z Special Unit successfully sinks Japanese ships in Operation Jaywick.

1944: June 6 – D-day – Allied forces invade France and push back the German Army.

1944: December 6 – Japanese special force Teishin Shudan attacks US bases in the Philippines.

1945: April 23 – Russian and US troops enter Berlin.

1945: April 30 – Adolf Hitler commits suicide, as he knows Germany has lost the war.

1945: May 7 – Germany surrenders.

1945: September 2 – Japan surrenders. World War II ends.

Glossary

Allies — countries and armies (US, Britain and its empire, France, the Soviet Union) that joined forces to fight the Axis powers (Germany, Italy, Japan)

amphibious (raid/assault) — military operation involving forces landed from the sea

artillery — large firearms such as cannons or rockets

battalion — military unit made up of two or more smaller units (companies or batteries)

commando — soldier trained for surprise raids and missions

D-Day — the day when Allied forces invaded France during World War II (June 6, 1944)

elite — a small powerful group with the highest qualities or skills

French Resistance — organization of French citizens opposing the occupation of France by Germany

frogmen — special forces who carry out missions using underwater gear

infiltrated — gradually became accepted as a member of an enemy group, for the purposes of spying or sabotage

landing craft — a boat specially designed to land soldiers and their equipment on a beach

limpet mines — explosive devices that grips to a metal surface using magnets

paratroopers — troops trained and equipped to parachute from aircraft

regiment — a large military unit, usually a number of battalions

sabotage — damage caused by enemy secret agents to make a nation's war effort more difficult

tactic — carefully planned military action

Victoria Cross — the highest British military award, presented to soldiers for extreme courage and bravery in the face of the enemy

Index